WHERE
DO
THINGS
GO
?

ALSO BY MARCY HEIDISH

Fiction:

A Woman Called Moses
a novel based on the life of Harriet Tubman

The Secret Annie Oakley
a novel based on the legendary sharpshooter

Witnesses
a novel based on the life of Anne Hutchinson

Miracles
a novel based on Mother Seton, first American Saint

Deadline
a novel of suspense

The Torching
(The Bookstore Murders)
a novel of supernatural suspense

A Dangerous Woman
Mother Jones, an Unsung American Heroine
a novel of a self-proclaimed Hell Raiser

Destined to Dance
a novel about Martha Graham

Scene Through A Window
a Medieval romance

Non-Fiction:
Who Cares? Simple Ways YOU Can Reach Out
A Candle at Midnight
Soul and the City
Defiant Daughters: Christian Women of Conscience

Poetry:
Too Late to Be a Fortune Cookie Writer
Burning the Maid: Poems for Joan of Arc

WHERE DO THINGS GO?

POEMS BY MARCY HEIDISH

WHERE DO THINGS GO?

Copyright © 2015 by Marcy Heidish

LIBRARY OF CONGRESS CATALOGING-IN-PUBLICATION DATA
Heidish, Marcy.

    p.cm.
    ISBN: 978-0-9905262-4-7
    Library of Congress Control Number: 2015955969

Cover: Poster Print of Jeanne Hébuterne (1898-1920) by Amedeo Clemente Modigliani (1884-1920); Public Domain Image; Design by Marcy Heidish

D&A (Dolan & Associates) Publisher
Printed in the United States of America
....
Second edition

FOR SAM

I have no time for hate....
~~ Emily Dickinson

So many things
You'd not have thought of
Until they were given.
~~ Jane Hirshfield

One does not live in the moment.
One lives in the whole history of one's being...
I have not dared to forget....
~~ Stanley Kunitz

CONTENTS

PROLOGUE

First May I Ask...

W here do things go?
The scissors in my hand
just yesterday, I think.
The tape in your hand,
only last night, wasn't it?
The TV remote control,
later found in the fridge.
The name of that actor,
you know who I mean and...
what was I going to say?

Why am I in the kitchen?
I knew when I came in,
looking for something,
it seemed to be crucial
two minutes ago
when I tried to locate
the can-opener
or was it the can
I wanted instead?

The Baby Boomers are
losing their car keys.
Is this a sign of distraction,
dementia, or age?
We worry, we wonder,
we leap to dire suspicions.
But here is one consolation,
fixed firmly in place:

Bright as new spoons
the distant past gleams—
Your first taste of ice cream
That first fall of snow
A sewing basket, red thread,
A porch swing, slice of sun—
all inked in our minds
to tell us, perhaps,
what really matters.

ONE

Crazy Collage

At random, I store these snippets of time,
mixed scraps of once-was, in my mind:

Waxy scent of Crayola Crayons, blue, rose, gold,
in my five-year-old fist; green sea of cut grass.

That brassy sassy tawny-haired girl, my friend,
tasting, with pride, a nugget of dirt in the park..

His head a white crest, old man on a bench,
feeding Hershey's Kisses to passing squirrels.

Or my uncle, proud of his scalp's pink shine,
conducting stereo music with his own baton.

Somehow I need each fleck of this crazy collage,
melted onto the walls of my own inner gallery.

My mother-in-law, a drudge all her long life,
in an old-style kitchen, in an old dying town,

lit up her walls with pictures of promise,
torn from the pages *Life* and *Look* Magazines:

The Breck Girl, palm trees, The Marlboro Man
movie stars, winged cherubs, a planet with rings....

In her kitchen, she shellacked these images
to a door where they made a lasting *decoupage*.

We all crave a glimpse of some visible glories;
this woman brought her choices to reality.

Perhaps this technique offers new ideas to me
I can add more images to my own internal spaces:

A snapshot of one pink sandal left on the beach
and a close-up drawing of a one perfect peach.

Changing Skins

Over time I've worn several skins,
peeled off, one by one, like husks.
I have shed them with some relief
and occasionally with reluctance
but some force is paring me down
to the marrow of what I must be.
I am changed, I have been altered
in later life; I don't know why.

When I squint, looking back,
I note the long trail of my footsteps:
more behind me, I think, than ahead,
and every few steps another husk.
Some of my walking companions
have left their prints beside mine
but several are blurred now, faded,
and others washed out with the tide.

I toss them my thanks and apologies
the way I throw salt over my shoulder,
an ancient way to ward off bad luck.
Those who are gone from me cannot
be recovered; I have to move on
to grow yet another suit of new skin.
I cherish the way that opens ahead
and somehow I know I must use it.

I will do whatever is asked of me now,
clothed in this skin I have been given,
lighter and thinner than any before it,
only enough for a shortened journey.
As I travel, I am charged to tell stories
and sing the songs I hear on the wind.
Where do all these things go? Listen.
Repeat them. They go on with you.

Prancing

Fires are burning in California.
Their smoke drifts like bridal veils
over Nevada's chapels.

Tires are skidding in Chicago.
Their screams ride the winds
to Iowa's cornfields.

Fliers are crashing in Arkansas.
Their planes scatter debris
over Tennessee's cities.

Meadows in Colorado are calm.
They spread through valleys
sunlit, yolk-yellow, where

the deer are playing touch-football.
They jostle each other and butt
a pine cone around near the trees,

then snort, feigning fierce attack
with their sprouting antlers
like boys in a solemn scrimmage.

A slice of sun halves the grasses;
elderly pines whisper cautions
in vain, as always, to the young.

Later, at dusk, one of those bucks
was hit by a car down the street
and, bleating, he bled; he died.

The driver, irate about his fender,
blamed the deer for the accident
but the buck had paused first.

Three witnesses confirm and agree
but we know this will happen again
when dusk blurs the winding roads.

So I hold that scrimmage in mind:
The deer leaping on delicate legs,
sporting, as designated, designed.
.
I want to honor the sunstruck days,
framed as they often are by the dark.

And in the dark, fires are burning.

Leaves

Dance.

Let your falling leaves scatter.
Don't pile them too soon.

The angel is here in a truck.
His baseball cap and his boots
make him look like a workman
but you know what he is.

His blower stirs all the leaves.
They rise upward like kites—
Paste their colors to the sky
before they drift down.

If a blue moose comes out
of the woods to watch you,
welcome him as your guest.

Whirl in the yellow confetti
while it's still with you.

Dance.

Dusk on Cheyenne Mountain

Evening deepens down to indigo
and takes into itself the pine trees;
melting needles, blurring branches,
finally dissolving every aged trunk,
until these woods, that sky are one.

Across a spreading sea of night
my house floats like a party hat,
a gaudy thing, a fragile thing, set
against the elegant simplicity of
black, unbound and bottomless.

Darkness washes over boulders,
over brush, over the backbone,
the shoulders and the skull
of this pensive mountain,
where time does not exist.

I hope for stories that repeat
themselves here if I can wait;
if I allow the darkness to reveal
what can't be heard at noontide:
the mountain's knowing voice.

Cupped in candlelight I sit
on my deck, hoping to hear it;
but not a word slides across the
eons to me until I lean down
and put out my own light.

Then I give myself over to this
place where silence speaks and
black is the rarest form of white.
Now I am one with the mountain
as we go into the ocean of night.

Vail, Colorado

Mountains
grip the sky's
wide hem
like giants
vying for
attention
and sun
is a gold
button on
a cloak
of thin
blue air
until fluid
shadows'
waves rise
to melt the
mountains
into night
darkness
hides the
glimmering
gold clasp
of the new
day's cape

That Moment

When it happens, don't deny what you see.
Don't force it to make sense or fit your mold
Allow yourself to be molded instead, let it be.

Near your mountain-home there are deer.
In the trees you sense one is waiting for you;
but as you approach, you see something else.

Its size is deer-like and so are its elegant legs
but the coat is lighter and there are no antlers;
only a single horn like a bone on its head.

You know what it is before you dare name it.
A unicorn has entered your garden's border;
its eyes liquid brown, its pale coat sleek.

Your teachers called such creatures "myths"
but you look at this face as it regards your own;
the unicorn breathes as deeply as you do.

The long neck arches like a swan's as it bends.
You reach with one finger to touch its head;
as if pleased, the unicorn bends lower.

You dare to stroke its horn, like a smooth branch,
as you speak lovers' language into its mane;
you offer your thanks, all you have to give.

A sudden noise rises from the woods' recesses,
perhaps a black bear or worse still, a hunter.
Ears flattened, the unicorn bolts away.

Where did it go? You know it will not return,
not today, not next week, not next year.
And you know you will never stop waiting.

Eating Words

Listen. Bears in the garbage again.
Unworthy of note for a house in the mountains
but worthy of note for a frustrated writer.

This time no orange rinds were consumed,
no crusts, no crumbs, no cremated asparagus.
The bears dined on "manuscript *marinara:*"
soaked in tomato sauce, seasoned with garlic
—the draft of a novel I could not get right.

Two hungry bears found it in our dumpster.
They pawed through my novel's insipid prologue,
munched on the soporific first chapters,
going on to devour some two hundred pages,
saturated in red sauce, too spicy for us.

I'd finally sent out my flawed manuscript
—and where did it go? It found takers
whose enthused reception was immediate;
you might call this reaction a rave review.

How to reward creatures who destroy shame?
Once I feared bears who can kill with one swipe.
Now I smile when I notice them, even at night—
"Thank you," I say, "For accepting my novel."

My Life on My Back

On moonlit evenings like this one,
purpled with the newborn dark,
I take the safe swamp-land trail,
walled for miles by rustling reeds.
There I tramp on spongy ground
with my whole life on my back,
until I know for certain I'm lost.
I can't hear the voice of the river,
my guide, so I must reach into
the skies for a light to lead me.
Lifting my hand to the North Star
I touch it, I trust it, I tap it;
the star opens up like a window,
taking me onto a different path
where the way is clear and the
life I bear on my back is blessed.

Night

It is late but the dark is young
the houses on this street
are closing their eyes
the trees shift in slumber
 in their murmured dreams

I sit within a bowl of night
conformed to its curves
where I wait for words
to spill into the bowl
if I remain silent and listen

for the sibilant sound they create
to signal their presence
they are quiet by nature
first heard in the mind
amplified by our daylight voices

but here in night's bowl the words
slip in like a whisper
outside a lover's window
even the hard words
with muscular heft enter this way

though I sit in the dark I watch for
the words' different colors
older than time fresh as new milk
not yet formed from the grass
sprouting now in this bowl of night.

Red Flag Fire Alert

When you're under a Fire Alert,
each object you own appears rare,
incomparable—a museum piece.

You see them all with intensity,
even the blue-and-white dishcloth
hung as usual by the kitchen sink;.

your desk lamp with its glass shade,
the one you cursed for its flickering,
now takes on the look of a lighthouse.

Every volume and all of their pages
now resemble the whole *Book of Kells*,
—or perhaps the famed *Magna Carta*.

If the order comes to evacuate now,
what will you take in two or three bags?
How to select which friend to save?

Documents, medicines, credit cards—
but what of that needlepoint pillow
you always hated until this moment?

China and crystal lose their sheen
next to photos of Chartres Cathedral
or a painted giraffe carved in Ghana.

Monks warn of "attachment" to things
but "things" are not what you own—
they are signposts marking your history.

You need such markers to point your way
even if they're a bit chipped or broken.
And so you keep vigil; you watch the wind.

In a Doctor's Waiting Room

Is this one of Hell's outer circles
Dante had not yet discovered?
Rows of blinding orange chairs
rows of heads snapping to the left
when an interior door cracks open.

A name is called but not yours.
You are waiting waiting waiting.

The television is set to cartoons
loud enough to be heard in Madrid
magazines droop like limp leaves
you fill out forms with old pens
topped with new plastic flowers.

A name is called but not yours.
You are waiting waiting waiting.

A brain's replica rests on a shelf
under a child's framed drawing
of daisies with faces in a red pot;
noise and color deny the presence
of invisible doctors cloistered within....

A name is called—it is yours.

You go to an examining room
where you discard your clothes
in favor of an open paper robe.
But where did the doctors go?
You sit waiting waiting....

Where Does My Education Go When I Die?

Will my Jane Austen paper
evaporate when I expire?

Or my simplistic study of the
Shakespearean sonnets?

What of my essay comparing
Giotto with Georgia O'Keefe?

Or the contrasting themes of Ibsen,
Strindberg and Woody Allen?

All I knew of molecular systems
has already gone into the ether

with algebra and logarithms
(though that's no tragedy).

But how can I lose my copious
notes on *A Tale of Two Cities?*

May I please take with me to God
the works of Emily Dickinson,

Beethoven, Monet and my thesis
on the obscure Biblical heroines?

Will *The Red Badge of Courage*
be waiting for me if I get to Heaven

or will I pace Purgatory for eons,
conjugating eccentric French verbs?

Paring Apples

for Eva

You pared apples
with a twist or two
of your deft wrist,
whenever you
incised the brittle
blood-red skin
of a Macintosh
into one thin
trailing curl.

Without a pause,
you carved spirals
of the fruited flesh,
shaving it layer by
layer, like a mesh,
as the apple's girth
swiftly diminished,
exposing the core
when you had
finished.

As I grew, I watched
this ritual with awe
but I didn't grasp
then what I saw:

Time's action on life,
swift, subtle, silent
as a scalpel or a knife,
peeling off years,
layer after layer
day by day by day,
until we are honed
to the bone.

Island Vacation

From our flat roof we
watched the bay spread
like a field of blueberries,
noon-lit, barely rocking.
Then, over your shoulder,
I saw paired white wings
open wide as an angel's
approaching embrace;
maybe the bird was only
a seagull—or maybe not.

Beyond the pale wings
was the bleached peak
of the neighbor's house
and above it, hovering,
a cloud like fresh snow,
airborne and triangular,
as white as the peak,
as white as the wings,
as white as your shirt,
as kind as your face,
all framed by the bay.

So precise, so definite,
this picture, I knew,
was inked within me,
tattooed on my soul;
an instant the size of
a raindrop, containing
that sweep of a view,
the brightness of sun,
the blue of your eyes
I look into each day.

How many instants
like this do we miss?
Where do they go—
or do we glance away,
ignoring what's small
as a priceless ruby?
Trillions of instants
wait for us in the dark,
without the wide view
without the white wings
or the blueberry bay.

The Last Trip

Where are we? Where are we going?
This is an unscheduled stop.
It's not on our itinerary.

The guides smile.

Why this detour from the mapped route?
We highlighted it in yellow.
That is not Lake Como.

The guides smile.

When did this trip change its direction?
No one told us upfront.
Please stop the bus.

The guides smile.

What kind of tour are you running here?
We don't like surprises.
Let's call it quits.

The guides smile.

Why don't you offer a clear explanation?
We wanted a holiday.
May we get off?

The guides smile.

When was it ruled we must go all the way?
We missed that part.
Okay then, onward....

The guides are still smiling.

TWO

Hat Trick

Every season is a donation to us,
but if we lose track of these gifts,
we can count on reliable hats,
piled on each other in a hall closet.

Hats, like sundials, orient us
when we need brief reminders:
they tell us where we were,
probably when, perhaps why.

A straw hat means Summer, a felt hat
means Fall, Winter's woolen caps,
occasional Irish tweeds, and of course,
the silk one with roses: clearly Spring.

Each year brings more seasonal cues:
a top hat for a one-time opera gala,
the vinyl number from a wet April,
the white bridal bonnet with its veil.

Lend us one more March, even windy,
we beg, as hats pile higher each year.
Let us wear that ridiculous red thing,
a stocking cap, a whim from December.

As we add to these tall piles of hats,
we secretly hope to add more seasons
and months, even years, even days,
to the entire lengths of our lifetimes.

We want to believe in our durability,
reflected each season in headgear—
until a brim falls off, a crown falls in
and we stand at the closet, hat in hand.

Open Doors

The blue-eyed sky widens its gaze
at aspen trees wearing gold aprons
that sway above slender white legs.

The air tastes like almonds and ale;
in the breeze, hear a violin's voice
then a distant fanfare of trumpets.

Open your door to get the paper
and flocks of winged leaves fly in
to alight on the hallway's floor.

Split a chestnut for its scent,
dense, distinctive and dark,
a revelation of its earthy self..

Lift your windows to watch
the curtains swell and billow
like sails on a broad reach.

This is a time for openings:
minds and ovens and arms
packages, heavy drapes.

Fall can expand our view,
if briefly, of what is passing:
the splendor of a single day.

You may not see this again.
Poignant, potent, doomed,
Autumn cracks you open.

Passing Notes

A tumble of leaves
from the maples today
their blazing red piles
like small campfires
set by the roadside

The autumn sky is
a huge bell missing
its metal clapper
but so fiercely blue
it seems able to ring.

As I leave a store for
the small parking lot
I see a white card
on my windshield,
the only note visible.

Beneath the sky's bell,
I stand still as I read:
If you want good sex
just blink your lights;
stay and I will find you.

As a teacher I notice
the clear punctuation,
even a rare semicolon,
how perfect it is—
this graphic come-on.

I quit that lot, speeding,
my turn signal unused:
Is that a blinking light?
In the rear-view mirror
I see nothing, no one,

but my hands tremble
with shock, fear, rage.
Who was watching me?
I can't find out but safety,
as I knew it, has altered.

Under that fierce sky,
far from the parking lot,
I hurl the note into a pile
of flaming-red leaves
as into a raging bonfire.

A Cynic's Thanksgiving

How conceited it looks,
even headless, that amber bird,
the size of an over-ripe watermelon,
centered and settled on a tray,
it presides over the festivities.

Set off by an ivory damask cloth,
or sheets, perhaps orange plastic,
the long table is deftly arranged
so the iconic turkey holds court
even as it is carved by a blade.

Cranberries cannot outshine
this avian symbol of harmony,
unity and traditional thanks.
No wonder the table groans
under hope's expectations.

Strays and strangers meet
friends and family, as together
they dine on the guest of honor:
white meat, dark meat, a leg?
Choices don't spoil commonality.

The feast ends like the turkey,
now akin to a gutted building.
The bird's wreckage, removed,
leaves a gap in the holiday aura
and we wonder—where did it go?

Most of the men here retreat;
football and beer offer escapes.
The women clean up the kitchen.
Guests drift out into the night,
one by one, solo strangers again.

How we depend on our icons
to draw us and hold us together.
We've always needed our myths.
Next year we'll have two turkeys:
one to eat, one for posing, intact.

Cold Days

T rees sleep

in winter they rest
dressed in white.

What a relief to be
freed from producing

striving to flower
to grow, make fruit

the peer pressure
must be intense.

Earth itself rests
in a deep freeze

relieved of plants'
insistent demands:

corn crops' creation
the prodding of seeds

but we are buzzing
with seasonal needs:

snow boots, shoes,
blowers, shovels, skis.

Shopping and buying,
we may not remember:

winter is a cathedral
on its best days when

bare black branches
window the low skies

tall pines rise as spires
the sun is suspended

like a Presence Lamp
over an altar of snow.

Dusk In Greenwich Village

A chill day fades into the sepia
of fine print in an aging book;
its covers close on the afternoon.

Before the sun sinks into the west,
it gives us a rare flash of topaz.

Windows become beige silk panels,
trees disappear into dimming skies;
birds curl within their folded wings.

Across the street an empty house
dissolves into a deeper darkness.

Evening has an old library's feel:
leather, glue, lilac, stories, secrets.
My study's aura invites me to stay

but I draw the sitting room's drapes,
brew tea, lay a fire, get your whiskey.

The city's din rushes past us now;
You arrive, shake off the chill air,
report news I don't like to hear.

Outside sirens are screaming again;
until they subside, I bite my lips.

Why was I born in the wrong century?
Give me gaslight, flies, chamber pots,
—and quiet, civility, relative peace.

I feign interest in what you are saying
as I slip drops of whiskey into my tea.

Mud Time

I like this half-season
following winter when
the air is raw and gusty;
and the earth is unlocked.

Windshields are splattered
doormats look weary
daffodils push up inside
the coil of a garden hose

Wherever the ground
can form a mold, a matrix,
you see small wet dents:
muffin-tins of recent rain.

Look away, look again;
you glimpse a green haze
so ghostly it eludes you
when you stare too hard.

Here is a pocket of days
conducive to thought;
you can hear voices and
bells and returning birds

before saws and mowers
bite the air once again
before a flurry of cleaning,
before that rush of repairs.

Mud Time: honest and rough,
pulling hair, tugging hems,
prankish, antic and alive,
ending pale winter's torpor.

Spring

The daffodils failed to come up this year
but the ground is hazed with shy colors,
now laundered by clean morning light.

My lips part as if to taste this rare air
as palpable as a pound cake would be
but lighter than any frothy souffle.

As I walk mud paints my shoes red-brown,
the color of wounds, recent, serious, deep.
Spring, for me, is not about not eggs.

There is the circulation in all growing things;
the life-flow in forests and forsythia's blooms,
the heartbeat of this globed earth itself—

and the cuts of a vandal on one of my trees,
its two pierced limbs spread wide like arms.
I see the Cross in this bleeding oak tree.

It reminds me: this pink-and-gold time
is also a season of blood and sacrifice
before the resurrection of summer.

I Hate Summer

For me it begins in shopping centers:
Barbeque fluid and Briquettes appear
and the familiar becomes unfamiliar:
inflatable, flotational or collapsible.

Sun screens and after-sun creams,
door screens and window screens
mosquito and moth screens are sold
by the thousands with folding chairs.

By June magazine covers lure us
with photos of models, pool-side,
with Band-Aid bikinis, waterproof
lashes and long mermaid-hair.

Those women can run on sand,
ignore flashbacks from *Jaws,*
read with ease in bright sunlight,
catch a Frisbee and tan, not burn.

Unlike me they don't hate summer;
it's probably their daughter's name.
I have come to admire such ladies,
glistening nymphs I shall never be.

In August, makeup melts on my
face and in my purse and milk
products spoil before I get home.
Mold appears; mildew threatens.

Libraries close at eccentric hours
as do shops, banks and museums.
Boaters and psychiatrists vanish;
parasols appear in pink drinks.

Summer features light fiction,
light dinners, light movies, and
perhaps a little light sex tonight.
Father, a light sermon, please.

To cope I stay in and repeat a
promise from *The Great Gatsby:*
"Life starts over again in the fall."
As summer's Scrooge, I agree.

The Hour of Blue

As a parting gesture,
like a bride's tossed bouquet,
the fading sun scatters
petals of light over my desk,
the teapot's plump curve,
a strainer, the bowl of a spoon.

This is the hour of blue.
Here in my dimming study,
I turn on the lamp with
a half-moon cream shade,
ruffle the papers before me,
and go on thinking of you.

I imagine you coming in now,
silent, glancing at my face,
then quickly looking away,
you study the floorboards,
waiting for me to speak first
but I am not yet quite ready.

I see us in the silence together
as if we share a swimming pool
where we must move out of
the shallow end and go deeper;
where we can dive underwater.
How long until that feels safe?

We will begin the swim soon,
three times a week this autumn,
unless you drop out or drown
before I can give you new words
in a basket I've woven of air—
the one I'm preparing today.

You, my students this semester,
wait with me for our course to begin.
We only know each other's names,
but next week all this will change.
You will be real to me and I, to you,
as our first class meets in Room 222.

Fishing On Holiday

Laugh with me now a lot or a little
as we sit on a wood-warm deck by the bay
to watch a couple in a small shiny boat;
the water calm, a cloud-dappled mirror
reflecting a bowl of salty blue skies.

The woman, in joyous awe, we assume,
laughs as she reels in a long silvery fish
while the man in the boat urges her on.
The air is so still their voices sound near,
so close we hear the woman say, "Wow."

Now we lean into the couple's laughter.
palpable as an actual person beside us,
our voices woven with those on the bay.
So let's laugh just a little or maybe a lot,
even if we lack a small boat, a big fish.

We don't need them to fill this moment,
one of those startling flashes of grace,
not requested, demanded, or deserved,
but real as the taste of brine on your lips.
Our gratitude is, once again, overdue.

Light

Tented by sun I stand watching
a doe nursing her hungry fawn.
They were two when they came,
balletic as they leapt into meeting.
Now, fitted together, they are one,
forming their own primordial unity,
simple, graced, basic, miraculous.
Whenever I see this natural act,
it appears both eternal and new:
humbly iconic: mother-and-child.
I don't move until the deer move,
the doe first, the fawn behind her.
After they vanish into the trees
I remain in their tent of light.

THREE

Once Upon a Time

Once there were places called bookstores
—perhaps you've not heard of them yet.
They were lined with shelves made of oak;
walls of shelves filled with actual volumes,
the colors of butter and brandy and blood;
they stood side-by-side, proud spines out.

Books smelled like leather, paper and glue,
mingled together like fragrant pipe smoke.
You could pluck a book from the shelves
as you would pick off a leaf from a tree.
Every book had real pages you could turn,
and turn again, turn ahead or turn back.
Each page held an orchestra of words,
waiting to release hidden music to you.

You could buy a book to hold in your hand,
feel its weight, sense its heft, its *gravitas*.
Soon you'd start haunting that dim shop
with its thousands of pages in one place,
but few stores now offer such a pursuit.
One day, perhaps, museums will replicate
an old-time bookstore, even older than I,
so you could pierce the magic yourself.

Listen

Words curl in the air
all falling like leaves
unfurling green lives

they whisper secrets
laughing like children
then deeper rustlings

attend to their stories
as ripening peaches
cling to a tree's arms

watch words scatter
like October leaves to
spill in your pathways

winter's bare branches
are not stripped of words
these speak through birds

words tumble around you
as skies lean and listen to
tales they forgot to recall

the stars hear each word
ever invented and so they
will when we are long mute

this is how grace arrives
in a shower of word-leaves
God spoke them into being

At the Art Museum

Still Life with Peanuts

T hey dominate this framed composition:
peanuts, unshelled, shaped like thumbs,
in contrast with paired avocados,
greenish and smooth but not ripe,
centered by one stunted eggplant,
the traditional bottled red wine,
and in the painting's lower left quadrant,
an elephant's head with extended trunk.

Nude Descending into a Bath

W e see her back, long and graceful,
as she leans toward the steaming tub;
her tawny hair is drawn up in a knot
but several stray strands ripple loose.

Her skin is fair, touched with peach;
the lifted right leg is poised in the air;
the artist has caught her in motion as
she steps toward the waiting hot water.

The substance down her arching spine
and across her twin shoulder blades
is an earthy brown, thought to be mud,
though her hand, extended, is clean.

The mud-streaked parts of her form
are impressed with yellow straw;
these suggest the figure has lain nude,
perhaps in a barn, for a roll in the hay.

The Bakery

Its lights snapped on at four in the morning,
as they did for fifty-one years in a neat row,
six days a week except Christmas and Easter.
The town's generations came to this bakery
for bread, rolls; cakes for weddings and wakes.

But people came for more than baked goods.
In the stern, severe silence of the shop,
nurture was kneaded, comfort became cake.
Twin sisters, both mutes, did all the work here;
their concentration, intense as snipers or saints.

When you bit into their bread, you bit into life;
you tasted each sisters' persistence and passion.
The twins' faces bore the patina of aged frescos,
but their hands and arms were still powerful,
shaped and strengthened by their daily labor.

In a thick yeasty silence, the two mute women
created their baked goods, always from scratch.
They frowned as they kneaded stubborn dough,
the makings of what would soon be transformed.
Their tenderness showed when they iced sweets.

Nephews and nieces worked the shop's counter,
sending the jingle of coins through the air.
When customers came, the door's bell clanged.
The twins never looked up; their focus was fierce,
their trimming was ruthless; slicing, surgical.

Under their hairnets, the sisters' expressions
fit warrior angels, the Furies, the Valkyries,
but when presenting a cake to a customer,
the twins' brown eyes were paired chestnuts;
smiles cherishing their creations—and you.

All the same, why bother with custom baking
when you can have ten Twinkies in a trice?
Is the taste really that different in the end?
The sisters' customers began to decrease:
there were shorter lines at the bake shop.

The twins' work told us of earlier times
when a craft was proud, precise, personal.
In that era, the sisters lived their lives.
When the bakery closed, they vanished.
Where did the sisters go? No one knows.

Sacred Stones

Let me be an old rock-wall in an Irish field;
stone laid on stone by hands long gone to dust;
that lingers beneath the accepting black earth.

Let me lie near to such earth, once, only once,
a staunch wall so ancient its age is unknown;
its rocks great gray bells, poised to peal, to toll.

Let me join the boulders set together tight as
knuckles on a giant's two clenched hands and
feel the sweat of those who hauled me there.

Let me border planted fields, their greenness
a thing you taste, you smell, and in the nights
you hear the deep breaths of sleeping crops.

Let me set off holy ground where men fought
and bled and died and left their broken blades
to mingle with the dust left under the earth.

Let me say I survived the Great Famine and
its walking skeletons who crawled and fell here,
their mouths stained green from eating grass.

Let me sit and watch the circling of centuries,
processions following the coffins and the brides;
priests blessing seeds and harvests and growth.

Let me catch the sun and bathe in the rain and
turn to gold for one brief moment at noontide,
as a spring breaks through an earthen crust.

Let me never die but wait to witness all life
until in the watching I become it and slowly,
gladly, gracefully allow myself to wear away.

The Bog
County Offaly, Ireland

Here the earth is stitched
to sky. Here the world
begins and ends. Here
a poet found his life and
it is here he chose to die.

Follow him. Take the road
from town as day fades and
amber light slants across
that sea of green-brown
peat lying open to the sky.

Go and wait. Something
will happen. Once a lake-
bed, then a marsh now
acres of moss, a bog will
show itself at its own pace.

Mind how you go. Mires
quake near silver water
strewn about like mirrors
in the turf where centuries
of laborers have worked.

We burn the turf as fuel
for the living but the dead,
long-preserved, also lie
below our feet. Haunted
and serene is this place.

Skirt the white lace of lilies
and green sedge. Look up.
Herons wheel overhead as
the bog spreads, raw and
rich, reaching beyond time.

The Tea Room

They were always there by four,
seated on a banquette by the wall,
each woman alone at her own table,
with her own tulip-shaped glass and
beside her, a small sleek bag from
Saks or Bergdorf, Bendel or Tiffany.

I watched these single ladies from a
table for three: my aunt, her mother,
myself, with their recent purchases.
They sipped Earl Grey tea and both
nibbled on—what else?—Lady Fingers.
I was permitted an ice cream sundae.

As a child, I was taken to tea rooms
two Saturday afternoons a month.
I never felt I was part of the scene:
elegant, hushed, plush, dim, elite,
scented by Orange Pekoe and *Joy*.
I was there to learn manners, think,

but I saw myself in a secret role
—as a deceptively innocent spy.
Bored by my chaperones' gossip,
I studied the ladies who sat alone
and envied their pastel drinks,
each with a Maraschino cherry.

Most of the banquette's ladies had
refills as they examined their bags,
refreshed their lipstick and stayed
in separate globes of sealed silence.
At times they smiled to themselves.
When we left, they were still there.

Now, decades later, that tea room
is gone and others are disappearing,
while I sit in a café with a cappuccino
and an open book on my sticky table.
There are other lone women like me,
some with books, laptops and wine.

We are not unhappy, we solo women:
the heirs of the lone tea room ladies.
I know now what their drinks were:
Whiskey Sours, hence the smiles,
and the bags held cheering trifles:
a Tiffany pen; a compact from Saks.

What a gentle way to end the day,
with a drink and a trinket and peace.
No one to please, no familial tugs,
no household crises, no tensions.
I'd pitied the tea ladies; my mistake.
I smile at my second cappuccino.

The Ladies' Room

Each word is a bead from a broken necklace
dropped, one by one, on the Ladies' Room floor.
How awkward to meet there, looking in the mirror,
how awkward we are as if we're still seventeen.
.
After forty-one years of silence, we speak of rain.
Our laughter is a deflated balloon losing its lift.
We hadn't known each other well, but well enough
to drop more bead-like words onto the silent tiles.

I didn't attend high school reunions you planned;
you were angry, still are, perhaps, can't let it go,
and I can't explain how I suffered through school.
Why does that still leap like a demon between us?

Who are you now, after a lifetime of changes?
And I? Not the girl I was, never quite fitting in.
The silent floor seems to expand until it's a field;
Across it, we toss our civilities like cotton balls.

In life's final decades let's quit high school games
and slog through that muddy field to touch hands.
But we are afraid to take those crucial first strides.
We part in the Ladies Room of a Five Star hotel.

Good Samaritans

Don't we all run past that man in the ditch,
and try not to look, more often than not?
Even so we think of him, that's the hitch.
Who is he, anyway, a tramp or what?

No one has the time to rescue strangers
and if one does there are legal angles,
not to mention a fair chance of danger;
best pass on that complex little tangle.

Some passerby stops and stares down
into the ditch. Should one of us go?
But the fallen man could be a convict
or a terrorist, a thief, who knows?

At last, we decide to act, not hesitate,
but the ditch is empty; we're too late.

Simple Gifts

This image comes to me often:

A square wooden table, hand-made.
One squat wooden chair, rough-hewn.
A loaf of bread, a fish, cupped wine.

This memory is one we all share.
Distant ancestors summon it for us.
Children will recognize it one day.

An image so simple, so vital, so spare
undergirds our timeless connections.
Why complicate it? Just take a seat.

The table extends its length now.
Other hewn wood benches flank it;
add more loaves, fish, poured wine.

Some crucial element is still missing.
The table is spread for a banquet—
but the invited guests do not arrive.

Birthday Table

I remember a birthday party, not mine,
where a boy fell asleep at the table,
his cheek on a slab of brick ice cream.
When he awoke to blow out his candles,
his face was striped with three flavors:
strawberry and chocolate, and vanilla.
Annoyed by his rest's interruption,
he cut the cake and resumed his nap.

That small boy had his sixtieth birthday
this year and his attitude was similar.
Confronted with all those tiny candles,
studding a long barge of tiramisu,
he blew out each flame in one go.
Never smiling, he halved the dessert,
then retreated to his private study,
pillowed there with a fifth of whiskey.

May we petition Congress right now
for a nationwide ban on birthday cakes
bearing more than ten lighted candles?
This custom, begun in remote antiquity,
is outdated, outmoded, outrageous to
those who need no reminders of age.
We need reminders of our inner youth.
One candle will do. Hold the tiramisu.

The Earth

You remember our names
while you bear our weight
and turn us toward the light.

We tread on your scalp
yet forget you are there
beneath our expressways

and cities and sunflowers
seas and soldiers and
your daughters and sons.

We plow you and mine you
and tunnel through you till
we think we're your ruler;

you always knew better and
though we err you take us
into yourself dust to dust.

Watered with blood and
drenched with our sweat
you sustain rebel children

and keep for us what we
cannot or will not recall
except in a dreamscape

where we call you "Mother,"
and when we say this
we know who you are.

Changing

The sky is trying on different silks
dyed purple, indigo, charcoal gray.
I wonder if a storm is coming or if
the designer was deeply depressed.

Perhaps it was the fickle Muse who
ordered these dim funereal colors.
They may be quite sophisticated,
a hot new trend I may have missed.

If these hues appear in the sky
for more than a week psychiatrists
will have full patient schedules;
pharmaceutical stocks will rise.

Or maybe we will get used to skies
tinted the colors of plums and guns
and change our wardrobes to match.
But as soon as we invest in darkness

the skies will shift into another mood,
replete with peach and gold and topaz.
Trend-setters will empty their closets
and the world will wear yellow again.

Cemetery Lunch

for Anne

W e lunched on a tombstone
throughout that hot summer.
Fish and chips, I remember;
you carried it all in a basket.
The tombstone, long and flat,
was the right size for a table.
Others, too, picnicked nearby.
in Boston's historic cemetery.
"Do the dead mind?" I asked.
You said, "They're *appalled.*"
We decided to stay anyway.

You, my first editor, smiled.
Your flinty eyes saw things
I missed or chose to ignore.
At seventy-five, you were fit,
gray, tall, thin; a sapling.
At twenty-five, I was not fit,
a fey small-boned redhead.
What an odd pair we were,
bound tight as twin sisters,
lovers of books and words,
haunters of musty libraries.

You ate steak, drank gin,
talked tough when needed,
smoked small black cigars.
At our gravestone lunches,
you never spoke of your life
as your fingered the grass.
"I'm acclimating," you said.
Three days later, you died.
No one knew of the cancer
racing through your body;

you'd chosen to go on alone.
No graves are open now
in "our" historic cemetery
but I still think of you there.
And I still see us together,
alive, lunching at that tomb,
laughing, appalling the dead.

Meditations on a Mystery

No one notes a fifth element:
Music, a manifestation of water.
These two can envelope us wholly
but can't be caught in your hand,
grasped in a fist, stashed in a bank.

They take many forms, this pair,
reaching us by various conduits:
pipes of shepherds and plumbers;
jazz men, rain, Indians drumming;
the rhythms of surf and concertos.

Music, like water, can bathe you,
flood you, lure you into its depths,
or teach you to let go and float.
Water, like music, slakes thirst
and can soak you, body and spirit.

Water is far more than H20—
music, far more than a C sharp.
In the end, you need them but
cannot define them completely;
they're part math, part magic.

Why not call music an element?
This is deserved, it *is* elemental.
Like water, it has power over us,
from a chord's crash to la-la-la,
storms to tea, they are Mystery.

Retirement Home

Each night I walk home in my dreams.
Exactly how many steps is that, I wonder?
There must be a number, an actual count.
A hundred, a thousand steps in my sleep?
All the time I walk that unmeasured mile
I am taking slow and deliberate strides,
mud drying on my hem and on my shoes—
shoes and hem and mud I see with a clarity
that only comes at certain moments of
strong sunlight, catastrophe, or grace.

I see my town begin, houses tufting up
like brown and yellow mushrooms near
the water which I smell before I see it.
I stand there on the rocks with the salt
candying on them and I feel strong then
unwearied and unhurried, but I know
there is somewhere I must go, must be.
Pulse quickening, I turn to the town but
the town, my town, is no longer there.
When I comprehend that, I wake up.
I look about me; where do things go?

I rise, wash myself and dress. Habit.
How else to start the day I do not know.
I've done this for the fifty-one years
since I was married, a girl of twenty.
That time belongs in another life.
That girl had a body smooth as glass
and I have a body heavy as dough.
Too many children, I have been told.
Well. Who is there to notice it now?

Up Near the Ceiling

Aman plays a harp in the hospice.
Each string has a voice all its own
and together, in chords, rills and runs,
they speak a mysterious language
only the dying can understand.

As they sink to lower levels of sleep
all inch away from the animate world
except this music they can still hear.
It strokes the sleepers' faces as their
fingers move in time to the notes.

Is it a B Flat that calls them?
They might hear more keenly now
and, dying, possess perfect pitch.
Maybe they hear celestial music or
riffs from a remembered Big Band.

Are their spirits up near the ceiling
where the dying can gaze downward
to view themselves as in a mirror,
or do they float on a lavender ocean,
foam-flecked and lit from far below?

Perhaps they drift back to childhood:
broad tables with baskets of peaches,
bunched sunflowers in tall milk cans,
the upturned faces of expectant plates;
in the background, the notes of a harp.

Suffering World

The sky is weeping on
the shoulders of houses
and the houses' thin skins

before there were houses
the sky was weeping
on the trees' green eyelids

before there were forests
the sky was weeping
on the skulls of stone caves

before there were caves
the sky was weeping
on the pain of all people

before there was pain
before there was Earth
the sky alone knows

before there was sky
there was God only God
and His breath of mercy.

Musical Medicine

The girl raises her flute
as if to kiss the new moon,
straightened into a line
by her fingers' enchantment;
her notes are a constellation.

The large hospital lounge
seems to contract around her;
twenty-two listening patients
lean toward her as she plays
tunes they might remember.

Her flute sings to the group
in this bright room where
bald heads move to the music
floating above yellow chairs.
Moon River will be next.

In this place with the music
are wheelchairs and IV drips,
walkers and oxygen tanks
but the music erases them,
if only for an afternoon's hour.

What magic is this, I wonder,
watching the sick and the dying
allow their masks to fall away,
their eyes fill; fists unclench,
releasing their pain for now.

It is as if the flute's voice,
delicate, tremulous, light,
lifts heaviness. As it plays
all these patients are whole,
are healed, are who they were.

At the concert's ends nobody
moves, even the orderlies who
take the patients to their rooms.
"I'll be back," the girl says.
One man snaps: "But will *we?*"

She lifts the flute once again
for an encore, one more, another.
Her dark hair and her face shine.
The encores go on, with requests.
She plays until her fingers bleed.

Dawn

The night drains away
like ink poured into earth

the sky has the color of
a newborn's wide eyes.

It is day dawn dusk
at this timeless time

when a veil thins between
us and what lies beyond.

Thin places thin moments
are sensed seldom seen

they await you in silence
or appear unannounced.

Do not mistake them for
daydreams or fantasies

but you will demand to
know what is their use?

The same use as wheels
ever moving us forward

and roads speeding us
past rising horizons.

Miracles

The dark descends
with long black sigh
to cool the feverish air
moistening dry ground
with its maligned mercy

in night's darkest core
in its secret marrow
hidden from daylight's
long probing fingers
its unblinking eyes

miracles open like night-
blooming flowers often
unseen understood
but they scent the air
before we notice

they blossom while
we pass their borders
and smell their perfume
tonight we can't guess
when a miracle opens

like the night-blooming
flowers scenting damp
air under our windows
as we close the shutters
and put out the lights

FOUR

Finding the Core

With sturdy ropes we weave our nets
immense as the earth or small as a knoll
our art is passed on so no one forgets
how strong we must be to bear souls.

This is the way we can carry them lest
one tumble out and crash on a shoal
we will not jar our passengers' rest
until we can get them into the Bowl.

Large as the moon, it holds our guests
whoever is weary, whoever is cold
we ask no names, all comers are blessed
here their lost lives will slowly unfold.

We, the world's mothers, offer our breasts
to the lost or the pained, youthful or old,
our strength equals a wild ocean's crest
so we can lift those we want to enfold.

This is not heaven nor hell nor a jest.
All who are here can sharply behold
their own lives, at the worst, at the best,
so they may strip down to a core of gold.

That First Quilt
For Kathleen

Burns can be healed,
even third degree burns,
with grafts and stitches,
time, craft and care.

When someone burns me
I go to one of my friends
and she gives me skin,
a tiny slice from her back.

I give her raw honey and
aloe vera for her wound.
When someone burns her,
she comes running to me

and I give her some skin,
a small spot from my arm.
She gives me witch hazel
and fresh sterile gauze.

We form a patched quilt,
enlarged by more friends.
We stitch up each other
as most women will do.

We give each other skin
and needles and thread.
Why? *Life can kill you,*
a wise woman laughs.

In many societies,
menstruating women
were isolated together,
bound by their blood.

Tented or housed,
they told their tales,
mending each other,
sharing their skin,

until they finally did it—
together they patched
themselves into that one
great primordial quilt.

An Offering

Take me now
take me completely
breathe me into yourself
until I am no longer
a block of pale marble
awaiting the sculptor
in Carrera's quarries.

I pray to the artist
he circles and scans me
deciding if I am worthy
his quick eyes say Yes
he carts me to his studio
where I will be changed.

I offer myself to him
as he sits watching me
his gaze like no other
looking through stone
to the figure within
he alone can discern.

I tell him in silence
Carve off what I'm not
leaving just what I am
even if there is pain
from chisel and mallet
I do this for your art.

I try to sound brave
he seems to hear me
as his blows strike
my own dust is rising
he hums to himself
I try not to scream.

I prayed hard for this
but I am in agony now
I regret my old offer
until I bow and submit
I go inside the pain
until it finally stops.

The sculptor's hands
caress me all over
he uses soft cloths
smoothing my shape
but who am I now?
At last I'm revealed.

In a piazza I stand
based in a fountain
but not as a nymph—
No, I am a *dolphin*,
my lips a water spout,
my fate: Forever a fish.

Table for Two

She ties his shoes
He knots her scarf
She buttons his coat
He finds her gloves.

Now they leave home,
a one-bed apartment,
at a pace irksome to
younger pedestrians.

Her white-water hair
swims in the breeze
his tweed Irish cap
hides his bald head.

At a funeral parlor
they stop, entering
its plush dimness
for an appointment.

It doesn't take long;
their list of requests,
a church, some hymns,
is short and concise.

The sunlight's stare
is bold as they depart,
their affairs in order,
left in knowing hands.

Back at their home,
they cook together:
she dices the carrots,
he slices the codfish.

A small round table,
with candles tonight,
is an island of light
in the dim kitchen.

Set off by the dark,
their old faces glow
a bottle is poured
into paired glasses.

They look across
fifty years together,
lifting their hands in
a champagne toast.

Making Vows I

On a black beach, a night wedding,
lit by multitudes of tall thin candles.
The young bride and groom, barefoot,
are flanked by friends and family.
The sound of the sea is their music.
Abruptly the wind rises, gusting;
Every candle and taper goes out.
The wedding, half-over, concludes
in the darkness, without a moon.
The bride can't find the groom's lips;
there is no kiss to cap the occasion.
The minister offers a humorous quip:
All marriages really begin in the dark.
The couple does not find this amusing.
Hey, they know where they're going.

Making Vows II

In the garden of a Greek restaurant,
ten minutes before it opens for lunch,
a mature couple stands in the sun,
just the two of them in street clothes,
as they await the Justice of the Peace.
He arrives in a straw hat and begins.
The vows are made, a kiss follows;
"Opah!" The waiters throw flowers.
Before the couple sits down to lunch,
the JP leans over to offer good wishes.
He makes an experienced statement:
All good marriages start out in sunlight.
The couple finds this quite appealing.
Opah! They know where they're going.

At the Supermarket

Will the checker remember to bag the milk?
I need to get pitted prunes for my neighbor,
reduced-fat Swiss cheese, whole grain bread;
after that there's the whole Produce Section.

This market looks like a library
with shelves of boxes instead of books.
Fluorescent lights glare down on them;
no glow here from green-shaded lamps.
.
As a reference librarian I cannot help it:
I resent the boxes in come-hither colors,
the lighting, the Muzak, this weekly chore;
I miss the civility of volumes well-shelved.

Now the Produce Section offers its wares:
those aggressive spears of asparagus,
tight-fisted fruit, carrots poised to poke;
cabbages: a collection of severed heads.

Then, in Vegetables, I find a rare sight:
a woman who smiles at the avocados.
Gentle-fingered, she touches the beans,
then moves to the Beefsteak tomatoes.

I watch her place one on her open palm.
As if in blessing, she bends her head;
her white corolla of hair appears lit as
she turns her liquid gray eyes to me.

She sees my taut face, clenched hands,
tight line of a mouth and she smiles,
her eyes giving me the same look
they bestowed on all the vegetables.

I notice the number tattooed on her arm
as she marvels at the red fruit she holds.
Before she leaves, she eyes me again and
she gives me that cherished tomato.

Noon Light

From the porch steps
I see light shatter like glass
on my lettuce-green lawn.
The sighs of three pine trees
create a triangle of sound.

I like the sun-warmed wood
on these low porch steps.
Here I feel secluded and safe
as I lunch here with my cats
and most days, a few books.

The hand of calm covers it.
This always falls at midday;
a pause in time, a held breath,
as work halts in the country
for half an hour, maybe more,

Two men at work next door
are swiftly clipping a hedge;
they snip into my silence.
Soon the men are talking,
their voices loud and free.

when men eat bagged meals
in the shade of their trucks
before they return to roofing
or laying brick for a new wall
in the heightened noon glare.

They speak about women,
the types they like to see,
older women,"still lookers."
I stand, slow but startled:
This talk is all about me.

I gather up cat, sandwich,
and books to move indoors.
Once settled, I turn around
to look in the hall mirror.
My face, I note, has a smile.

Garlic

Iam breathing in Tuscany's hills,
at a round table on a sunlit piazza,
tasting red wine and pasta *al dente,*
amply sauced in garlic and butter.

Again I inhale and I'm in Provence,
beside a pond of green water lilies,
where outdoor tables bear plates
of veal sautéed in butter and garlic.

That sculpted bulb, diced, sliced,
or minced, can take me off to the
best eateries all over this planet;
I travel with my guide of choice.

I wonder at garlic's early discovery,
a humble white bulb grown in soil,
first decocted for curative dosing,
cleaning the blood, killing colds.

Looking back into ancient times,
I see an old woman, an herbalist,
stirring a garlic brew over her fire,
tasting the brew, and then—*ecco!*

How intimately we are connected,
despite distance and centuries,
by what we eat, cook, and crave:
nourishment for body and spirit.

We want food's sensual pleasure;
even more we want its comfort:
earth's fruits, created in mystery,
growing like us toward the sun.

One Word

A man is kissing a loaf of fresh bread
as he waltzes alone throughout the night,
sailing about the guest room's narrow bed;
he sings one word to the yellow lamplight.

In five languages he carols, "Thanks,"
wishing he could be more transatlantic:
Grazie, Merci, Slainte, Tapadh, Danke,
all sung as if each word were romantic.

In the safe house of a welcoming friend,
this man croons gratitude to the night.
His prison sentence has come to an end;
this fresh bread is freedom he can bite.

What once he ignored he wishes to bless:
this long loaf of new life, yeasty with "Yes!"

Kitchen Magic

In my modern kitchen
I glimpse my reflection
in the wide window
as I tilt a blue pitcher
to pour a long ribbon
of sleek silk-like milk
matching the kerchief
that covers my hair.

The image changes:
I am a young woman
in a Dutch painting
of a kitchen in 1662
where I tilt a blue pitcher
to pour a long ribbon
of sleek silk-like milk
matching the kerchief
that covers my hair.

I wait for children
who never appear
as I stand serene
in a slice of sunlight
pouring all that milk
my apron spotless
as is my gray tunic
showing my bosom...

Wait! What's wrong
with this picture?
Though I still pour
that endless milk
I am jerked back
to the year 2016
and my own kitchen
by my own children
hollering: "*Mom!*"

The Map

If this were a plane, you'd fasten your belt.
Turbulence rises at all teachers' meetings
held in our school's well-lit conference room.

I listen as you, Chair at Large, raise "issues."
Your red mouth is a taut line until it opens
to demean a student who is my protegé.

On you go, critical, caustic—petty, perhaps?
I see your terrain as a large jigsaw puzzle,
territory fitted together; that is your turf.

I envision this puzzle as a map of our nation.
While you talk, I extract Texas and Georgia.
You continue: Ohio and Oklahoma go next.

You're still finding fault: I remove Maine,
California, Montana and Washington, D.C.
As you go on, I extract all the other states.

Now I have the courage to defend my student.
When I look at you, I see a woman displaced.
Powerless now—you are without country.

Recognition

Regrets, those uninvited guests, arrive
for longer stays than many hosts expect
and if one should venture to contrive
exemption from regret he is suspect.

But which of us can blame such hosts?
Do we fail to see ourselves among them?
We would rather paint ourselves as ghosts
in a tableaux of shamed women and men.

Denial is the drug of choice for pain
and pain companions genuine regret
but age gives us the wisdom to reclaim
our human frailty, however imperfect.

Wisdom lacks glamor but it does live on
chanting within us like an antiphon.

A Place for Mistakes

Come one, come all, show yourselves.
I know you're there, I hear you breathing.
You have trailed after me for decades
like persistent Pinkerton sleuths and
I've tried to evict you from my dreams.
My efforts have failed, as you know.

I took you with me to the confessional
but the line you formed was so long
the ancient priest nodded off in the box.
I never received what I craved: absolution
We tried therapy next but you hid from me
and the doctor who took you for phantoms.

An abbess declared guilt self-indulgent.
A respected mentor told me to move on.
On good days I do, I have, and I will,
but on other days I can hear all your
whispers back there, comparing notes
as to size, weight, depth and damage.

What can I do now but welcome you
since denial, rue, and excuses fail;
even repentance makes you sneer.
Come, you rogues, show yourselves
in fierce daylight that reveals flaws,
pores, crows' feet, lipstick on teeth.

I want to look at you as you are and,
with reluctance, claim you as my own:
the wrong turns, disastrous decisions,
inflicted pain, craven choices, regrets...
(This is where the priest fell asleep)
I invite you in now—be my guests.

If

If you can float on a lake
fingered by air
if you can lean on the sea's
heaving greenness
if you can drift off on music
never visible

If you can float on night's
black buoyancy
you can ride on its edge
and sink deep into
its untouchable darkness
without holding on

If you can do this you can
rest in God's palm
unseen but firm as a new
mattress waiting to
bear your heavy dreams
even as you sleep

Convent Interlude

"*No* Holy Water on the electric blanket."
Mother Francisca, my good friend, laughs
as she shows me her convent's guest room,
spare and serene as it was ten weeks before.
Except the electric blankets; they are new,
as are the sisters' individual pagers clipped
to rope cinctures, or belts, on their habits.
.
This country convent, hidden by oaks,
has been my refuge for thirty-one years.
In the chapel I smell old stone and roses,
candle-wax, incense and furniture polish.
These aromas alone tell me where I am.
This place, I've known, is where I belong.
Here is the life I did not live, but desired.

I wonder how many lives I have missed.
One is a Manhattan life, as expected ---
social, sophisticated, including children.
Another life, another role, is humbler:
work in Kolkata, India, with the poor.
A painter's life is one more I wanted,
but not enough; it was left unfulfilled.

Perhaps we all have alternative lives,
alternative spouses, unborn children,
unoccupied houses, here and abroad.
If we went back to our crossroads now,
what, where, whom would we choose?
I ponder these questions at Vespers,
then text a friend on my cell phone.

Coventry Cathedral

Stark and skeletal,
the ruined cathedral,
like a great gray fish,
lies boned and scaled,
but majestic in defeat.

This roofless church,
open now to rain and sun
upholds gray-blue skies
where bombs exploded
on November 12, 1941.

Partial walls did survive
one night's storm of fire.
Left intact: the stone spire.
Fallen crossed beams are
marked, "Father Forgive."

In the apse noon prayers
are read and we, hatless,
humbled, honored, stirred,
join our voices to the sound
of abiding ancient words.

Praise and supplication here
lasted for nine hundred years.
A new sanctuary shines near
this, the old one, preserved
as remainder and reminder.

"The Lord be with you," the
priest says. "And with your
spirit," we give the response.
"Let us pray..." Yes. Let us
do that now. Father, forgive.

Lost and Found

The prodigal son finally returns,
bringing home his issues and his laundry
and our settled lives begin to churn
as we sense the onset of a quandary.

When the lost are found do we forgive them
or resent them? Their reflection of us
could reveal a tramp or a tragedienne;
distance seems a better course than trust.

But wait! In an ancient tale we witness
a father's tenacious and tender embrace,
overwhelming his son with forgiveness:
a child who crawled his way back in disgrace.

Mercy unites us in age or in youth,
defying logic but defining truth.

Erosion

Tell me once again
that I remain myself
though time is changing
me, crease by crease,
as evening takes a
living tree, branch by
branch, into invisibility.

Snows have sculpted
canyons of stone spires,
elegant, ecclesiastical,
while others have eroded.
A rock gets millennia,
a butterfly, one month,
and we—who can say?

In the glass today I saw
my grandmother, tall as
a tiger lily; she laughed.
Her eyes, mine; then gone.
She never saw a canyon;
darning her son's socks
taught her about erosion

She knew, as do the rocks,
erosion is not the enemy.
It's I, resisting life's cycles,
who erodes what joy is left.
So tell me I remain myself,
even creased, and grandma
laughed, forty years deceased.

FIVE

Death of a Friend
for Caroline

Ancient tradition asserts
the dead are transformed
into constellations or stars,
visible in the night sky,
watching over the living.

Modern tradition asserts
the dead are transformed
into ashes and dust to be
buried deep in the ground
or cremated as requested.

Irish tradition asserts
the dead, behind a thin veil,
may sometimes visit the living.
After you left, you told me,
"I'm here, hiding from emails."

In my own tradition I assert
the *living* are heavenly stars,
their spirits embodied on earth.
And yet I have looked for you
without finding a clue....

Where in God's plan are you now,
my oldest friend? Where did you go
with your crisp smile, loyal love,
whispers at concerts, wry wit,
logic, laughter, grace?

There is a hole in the sky
where you were.

Tiny Blue Chair

Iran from you when the madness began
and your face wasn't yours anymore
and you yelled "Go to hell" on the street

yours was the face I had always wanted
to see in my mirror one day some day
when I wasn't eleven years old anymore

yours was a dense emerald gaze
like a medieval maze that drew me
in until I thought I'd found the center

no one else had an aunt who was Paris
and perfume—and that oddity, in 1958,
power, with an office and a briefcase

you could hold fire in the quick flash of
your cigarette lighter and you drank
Scotch neat, like a man, I thought

in church I watched your etched profile
veiled by the tremulous membrane
of your lace mantilla and you smiled

you only wept on Good Friday when
we made the Stations together but
then you began weeping at mass

at street corners and cash registers
and near a gutter on Fifth Avenue
where you threw your wedding ring

frightened, I ran for help but I didn't
know "help" lead you to the hospital
the psych ward with no way out

I erased your face from my mirror then
afraid I might turn into you as I'd wished
but I did have one package from you

a tiny beaded wire chair, turquoise blue
made in group therapy, with a note
"God's here—please pray anyway"

I never saw you again, despite requests
what you left to me is everlasting:
unshaken faith and that blue chair

Celebration

A slender branch of chance
bends her way

this raw January day
when she hears

her tests are back and
all of them are "clear."

That word is a lamp hung
from the fingers of a tree

light on milk-slick snow
her face arms legs torso

until she is the lamp
the light the snow

Guilt

You never made time to know me
because you had wanted a dog
and I, after all, was only a fish—
suitable for a New York penthouse;
on that much your parents agreed.

Did you notice my shimmering fins,
or the sleekness of my gilded sides?
I swam with synchronized strokes
but you seldom glanced at my bowl
with its plastic "coral" and pebbles.

I doubt that you understood me at all.
Didn't you guess how lonely I was?
I hoped in vain for a companion
but you tossed me seaweed instead
and that powdered fish food? Please.

No wonder I died on your grandmother
who kept me while you were at camp.
She flushed me away with her guilt.
I got to float in Manhattan's sewers;
you got a talkative blue parakeet.

Courage

Its skin is what
you first note about
courage
never its core
nor its heft nor its form
but the peel the rind
the binding
itself of the juice and
the flesh of the fruit.

It is the skin
sealing the body of
courage
until it is needed and it
gives itself over to you
but it is a fruit
you seek in secret
and never name.

It is your skin
that is risked when
courage
is needed to fight
an enemy
be it death be it life
be it human in form
be it you.

Emily Dickinson

Imagine her at the top of the stairs,
a figure in white pausing for a moment,
perhaps wondering where she left her pen
or making mental notes for the next poem.

She is an Easter lily as she stands still,
then moves to the wooden desk in her room;
when she sits she becomes an open camellia,
her skirts spreading like petals around her.

Outside in her father's expansive garden,
Emily is a staunch fruit tree in full bloom,
instead of flowers she scatters her verse;
she grows poems, this word-tree woman.

I see her back at her desk, writing quickly,
her pale hand gliding, her pale sleeve
smudged with her homemade black cake;
lamplight casts her shadow on the wall.

Emily cannot foresee her posthumous fame;
at the moment she's watching a fire in town.
Her sister lies: "It's only the Fourth of July."
but Emily knows about fires, snakes, death.

"I have no time to hate," she has written,
"because the grave would hinder me...."
As Emily dies she teases Vinnie, her sister:
"Don't worry, it's only the Fourth of July."

The Soother

A tall tough tree of a woman is she
hair the red of autumn's maples
arms strong and supple as branches
a lilting voice and roughened hands

making the beds of restless sleepers
smoothing their ivory silken sheets
tucking their ends under each mattress
she erases creases in twisted linens

Each day, in silence, she soothes the
visible pieces this tormented house
as she eases glass splinters out of a rug
and retrieves a Ming vase thrown in rage.

With old newspapers she wipes wine
off elegant windows and calms
the panes with her own soft rags
until these surfaces clear with relief.

In the kitchen, she drenches her mop
in the mercy of water and cleans
angry scuff marks from the floor;
they yield to her ministrations.

with her broom, in the hall, she sweeps
away shards of an heirloom hand mirror
and opens a door to clear the tense air;
she empties her dustpan into strong bags.

When the troubled family returns home,
its calm surrounds them—for a while.
Tonight, more clashes, more clamor;
tomorrow, the soothing begins again.

As the woman-tree sits with the child
of this house, rocking and crooning,
in this narrow room for "the Help,"
she is surrounded by a great crowd:

Everywhere women are making beds,
mopping floors, erasing all stains and
creases, leaving rooms scented with
furniture polish and soap and grace.

This is the unseen legion of angels
that keeps the world from flying apart;
for the sake of the child in the picture
this labor, this daily healing, endures.

My Students

I look out at your faces
like rows of plates on display
in an old-fashioned dresser,
its top half, glass windows,
and when a truck passes by
the plates tremble together
but do not fall to the floor.

You look out at my face
and yours seem to tremble
behind the invisible barrier
hanging between us for now
and I wonder if my face
quivers while you study me
as if to ask hidden questions.

Your faces reveal them:
Will she like me? Will I pass?
My face may reveal to you
the same tacit queries:
Will they like me? Will I pass?.
It always happens like this
on the first day of classes.

How much can I give you?
How much will you take?
I can't guess what you need.
But I will learn from you.
Even so, I can never know
Where you will finally go.

Woman-Tree

Fierce and focused as a warrior's gaze,
searing as the bluest core of a flame,
is the passionate love for a child raised
as your own marrow, member, membrane.

Ferocious is the love that child returns,
finding one home in one figure, one face.
I am such a child whose loving has burned,
not with mere gratitude, but sheer grace.

More mother than other, you are the tree
to whom I am grafted, branches and leaves,
nor could Death ever remove you from me;
in my own greening you live as I grieve.

She who does not tear the baby in two
is truly the one who is mother to you.

Nora

Red hair flying, a banner behind her
long strides, long legs swinging out
her skin, milk scattered with cinnamon
rough ugly hands but large, comforting.

She had a way with her, I learned early
people stepped aside for Nora on the street
New York doormen tipped their hats to her;
worn coat, worn shoes, they didn't matter.

Nora was *someone,* you knew right away
no self-importance, she was a stiff breeze,
a current of air, a bit of fire to her as well
call her a "Mick" and she spat, fists locked.

Her eyes two blue sparks the core of a flame
no beauty, Nora, there was something else,
some shine to her, some kind of radiance.
Young, she had an older woman's authority.

Always there, her voice my earliest memory
its Irish lilt soon my own, poetic, quick, sharp.
quoting Yeats, she carried me on her left hip
I was never afraid whenever she held me

Who was she, this tall girl, nervy, tender,
never saying why she left home in Ireland
My father helped bring her over, so I heard,
of course there was talk she firmly ignored

Smart, quick, she ran a doctor's household,
complex, troubled, where she mothered me
as if I were hers; maybe I was, maybe I wasn't
but she wasn't just "nanny," that didn't fit.

Nora Larkin taught me how to tell time,
tie my shoes, say the Rosary, count to nine.
Hundreds of tales and verses were hers,
with her stern love, she left them to me.

The Pen

Nora is shining the doctor's silver.
The child, sneezing at the polish,
wonders, "Why keep this stuff?"

With one hand, Nora lifts a plate;
in the light, it floats like the moon
above the long kitchen counter.

Soup spoons between her fingers
glimmer like small constellations.
A tray takes on the glint of a lake.

"Your father will leave this to you,"
Nora, sighing, informs the girl.
"I've but a pair of pens to leave."

The girl's guess: "Your father's?"
Nora nods. "Oak. One for you."
A poet's pen: the girl is thrilled.

"The other? Who will get that?"
Nora pauses and looks far away.
"One day...someone special."

Decades later, after Nora is gone,
the doctor dies suddenly, instantly;
His daughter must sort his things.

In his office she finds a sealed box
long and small and unseen before:
Inside, she discovers the other pen.

Rejoice in the Ruins
for MKM

In your old Irish house
the dim white-washed walls
crumbling like stale bread
and the hearthstone cold

All we ever said and did
together in twenty years
is compressed into this
one stunning instant

this flashes through me
as a pin pierces paper
it holds the story of us to
an old pocked corkboard

so I stand in this ruin
where you began where I
reached the finish of my
own stubborn searching

for those plunging roots
that grew you and grew
me into a branching tree;
Nora, I somehow knew

there is too damn much
I never asked I never said
too much we did not do
and it can't be done over

I linger here regretting
this wreck of a house but
you would insist I rejoice
in the ruins not the regrets

"Respect these ruins and
remember these ruins—
these signs of survival,
stones marking our lives."

Inkwell

Nearly forgotten now, I keep my place,
stalling for just a few more useful years;
isn't that always the hope of the aged?

I saw the swift scribbles of centuries;
many fingers have hovered above me
as I opened myself to serve them well.

Once my kind filled every classroom,
defining all desks, refining all words,
even as fountain pens killed the quills.

Fast was our fall through time's floor,
inevitable though our passing was
but some value us still, even now.

One writer sees me as a magical font;
her pensive pen dips, a dowser's wand,
seeking a vein of words in my depths.

She is the inkwell, I want to tell her,
I just reflect who she is and will be.
We unite in the words we both see.

Ode to My Typewriter

O trusted one,
firm in body, nimble of keys,
humming, you waited until
I found the right words
to stamp on your ribbons,

like a soldier's decorations.
scarlet and ebony, no less,
even when I pushed you
through draft after draft.

I blew cigarette smoke
into your waiting carriage,
while I typed and retyped
one paragraph ten ways.

Even when your keys
abruptly flew into the air,
you were never stressed
as you endured repairs,

caused by my antic fingers,
drumming you late at night,
beneath that hot lamplight
but you never complained.

We were together through
countless reams of paper,
through fluid White Out,
chalk paper, cut and paste,

as we struggled on, trying
to write something new,
adding our own words
to the world's sum of words.

I replaced you under duress
when "hard copy" declined;
editors now wanted novels
on disc, so I betrayed you.

Yes, I bought that computer,
a laptop, a confusing machine,
a mere babe compared to your
mature expertise; I did you in.

Without you nothing is the same.
I lose my network connections,
the machine refuses commands,
and I must talk with technicians

who are not as patient as you,
whom I miss and remember.
If you could forgive me now
I'd take you back at a key's tap.

Awake
for poet Anne Bradstreet, ca. 1650

Full moon tonight
a silver plate in the sky.

Wind like surf
in the pine trees outside.

My pen a silhouette
cast on computer paper.

Think of women
of other centuries

who worked hard by day
to write by night

after the house
had gone silent at last.

Full moon then
a pewter plate in the sky

I see women
heads bent, hair down

in log cabins
and raw frame houses

as their quills
cast sharp silhouettes

on rare paper
precious and coveted

they must write
without any erasures

in the light
of their burning oil lamps

outside the wind
like ghosts in the forests

a butter churn
guarding the doorway

spinning wheels
still and silent for now.

Piles of chores
but writing rises within

and must wait
for night to release it

at the cost
of rest and restoration.

Worth the price,
such women would say.

Now as I write
voices speak from the past:

"Read this, please.
I leave you this piece...

but tell me:
Be honest, I must know:

Do you *really* like it?"

The Wizard

Do not anger him, this tough old man,
his skin leathery, his beard, peppered snow;
and those grey eyes of his: paired nail-heads.
In his small shop, dim even on fair days,
he roosts on a high stool behind the counter,
fronted by junk he's labeled his "buddies:"
toasters, alarm clocks, eggbeaters, lamps.
more in the back, all damaged or broken.

You Break It, I Fix It, his door's sign reads.
He salvages what looks to be past repair,
by what magic, what skill, no one knows.
His record is flawless and he works fast.
The man snarls or snaps when he speaks
but satisfied clients spread his reputation
as some magician with surgical hands,
wielding scissors and tweezers and pliers.

Never ask him about the framed photo
hung on the dingy wall just behind him.
"Not your business:" he'll growl at you.
The picture shows a platoon of soldiers
standing together in a Vietnam jungle—
enlisted men all, young, with their medic,
the faces unclear unless you get close;
no customer has yet earned that honor.

Each evening, just after closing shop,
"the wizard," as his neighbors call him,
retreats to his small flat up the stairs.
He cooks his supper on an old hotplate,
then climbs to the building's flat roof.
There he lies on his back and looks up.
In the stars, he sees buddies from Nam;
those men he could not save or repair.

Roma Grandmother

In a line of painted wagons you
were born. "On roads," you said,
"We lived, we died." A "Gypsy"
compania was your first tribe.
There you did and did not thrive.

At fourteen you ran into the dark,
leaving kin and that old man you
must wed—to Bucharest you fled
alone, never allowed to go home.

You sewed to pay your passage
sailing with a shawl and an icon.
You, frail as forsythia, firm as fists,
took your icon through Ellis Island.

Old when I was young, you were
doll-like and diamond-hard
smelling of paprika and peaches
you sewed my father's "breeches."

Now I face aging and think of you;
I am ashamed to admit what's true:
You journeyed into the Unknown
and I fear traveling to God alone.

The Icon

The icon explained all things in her life,
she believed, and perhaps she was right.
It was as holy in her apron pocket as it was
in its nook in a Bucharest church, she said,
because God loved the humble and poor.

It was only a small Madonna and Child but
the icon led her on as she fled Romania.
Now when she sets the icon on a high shelf,
she pulls down the church like a great tent
over her and her home and her children.

All she ever wanted is here in one room:
the checked tablecloth lit by oil-lamps,
eggplant frying on the two-burner stove,
her magical Singer sewing machine and
her tall son studying on the fire-escape.

Her husband, a "rag man," worked hard
but it was she who put food on the table
from her small store beneath their flat.
Once foreign, she's now proudly American;
a stolen Romanian icon rendered her so.

She watches the play of lamplight across
the icon and whispers thanks and, always,
repentance for her theft long ago, far away.
Her American son looks up from his books
and comes through the window to supper.

The Rag Man

Slung over his shoulder
hung his rock-heavy bag;
he walked the back alleys,
calling and crying his song,
"The Rag Man's come,
bring now to me rags."
Housewives called back:
"The Jewish man's here."

Built small with a big
voice and a big load, he
trudged the streets of
New York's South Bronx.
Slowly he gleaned scraps
of torn worn-out material.
At day's end he sold these
to rich men in fine suits.

He always saved a scrap
for his frail young son:
fabric with color and form:
roses, plaids, and stripes,
checks and ripe cherries.
At night his wife stitched
these pieces together—
in time, they made a quilt.

Sam, the "rag man," believed
in family, work, America,
and the New York Yankees.
He didn't believe in luck or
drinking or gambling or God.
When he left the old country,
he left his home and religion,
never regretting his choices.

He labored for the future of
his children, not for himself.
Their destinies were his life;
he bore his rag-bag for them.
At fifty-four his heart quit.
He died under his creation,
the quilt, with his youngest
son and his wife at his side.

My father recalled this clearly.
He told me the story of the
weary "rag man" named Sam,
gone before his favored son
became a healer, a surgeon
—long before I was born.
Even so, I hold Sam close;
his quilt is here on my lap.

Grandparents Go

They are starting to vanish
but their eyes still watch me
from that old wooden frame,
once brushed with mock gold,
where they have been housed
for half a century, as I recall.

Sophia and Sam float together
on the crest of a spreading cloud
where a Bronx street used to be,
grounding them, giving them life;
now they look more like spirits
waiting to enter God's Heaven.

All I have of them is that photo,
with their tall son behind them.
Young, strong, he was my father,
still a medical student in 1928.
I should get that picture restored
before the family's clothing fades,

leaving them disembodied but
vigilant, watching the grandchild
they never knew but still observe.
After my father's death, I hung
that picture on my study's wall;
each day I note it and neglect it.

One day I'll look up with a shock
to find three pairs of eyes on me,
asking where are their jawbones,
folded hands, mended collars?
I will lack answers or excuses
as I return their enduring gaze.

The Fire Escape
For my Father

He lay on that skeletal stretcher
where he tried to glimpse stars
through the city's hazed glare.

In Harlem's harsh summer heat
he slept outside on his fire-escape
above the gushing fire hydrants.

On this metal raft by the window
he studied at night with a flashlight
until his mother woke to call him in.

Downstairs was her "Notions" store;
Below, other boys played stickball,
shouting, sometimes fist-fighting.

A skinny white kid, son of immigrants,
he had little time for street games;
life was Mom's store and his studies,

and always, his refuge, the fire-escape:
he plotted his own escape there, never
forgetting it once he got out of the slums.

Later, he saw himself as that "balcony"
where he grew tall, grew up, grew tough
enough to forge a whole different life.

The fire-escape taught him to endure
until, as a doctor, he promised the sick:
Above the city there really are stars.

The Surgeon

Cleansed
by submersion
in its nightly
bath of darkness
the tall tense city
stretches toward
the yawning dawn
as its grid-work
and its towers
glass steel stone
dress themselves
in shades of copper
deepening to bronze
while a young doctor
runs down the stairs
in a hospital to an
operating room
five high floors
above the city's
gleaming streets
where the surgeon
gowned and gloved
tells a nurse to
take a step back
before he straddles
the operating table
to wrest from a man's
throbbing stolid chest
an icepick

Sands of Time

"Women made the oldest known cave art...."
The Smithsonian Magazine, 10/09/13

When the tide is out and the beach is still,
I set my firm handprint into the moist sand.

This is who I am, distilled, I tell the ocean.
Here is my signature, my salute, my sign.
.

My hand joins hands with countless others
who left their own prints in moist earth.

They form an endless chain of greetings—
a connection we hand over and hand on.

This chain, then, could be an eternal spiral,
turning backwards and forwards in time.

It leads to the ancestral cave women
who left their own handprints on rock,

perhaps to sign their fabled paintings,
that live on after thousands of years.

Touch me, I say, *you who defy time,*
may our handprints reach each other.

I glance up now as the tide rushes in;
flecked green water overlays my print.

The water is thinning now as it recedes,
somehow leaving my deep print intact.

In the afternoon's fading light I peer at it;
Do I see another print within my own?

A Candle

Flame leaps to wick
brief curl of smoke
a white waxy scent

and a new life begins
its long slow descent
into waiting oblivion

or perhaps an ascent
of a luminous bloom
from one study stalk

or light's mystery in
the form of a flag on
a pole we can grasp

or fire's inspiration
about to ignite ideas
onto a waiting page

or a simple wick's stick
lit by one simple woman
in a far simpler time

Inventories

Houses crowd my past
like chairs strewn on a
spare November beach.

I've left ten roofs, two hearths,
twelve beds, four patios,
and seven states, East to West.

A pilgrimage, perhaps? Or my
last try at finding Oz? Now I can
claim many roots—and none.

All merge into a single voice, a rich
contralto, and this, in turn, blends
like distant music into distant skies.

Now my home is a tin archangel,
hammered to a simple board,
long-time guardian and friend,

and the figure of a bird, hand-carved
twenty years ago from a hefty gourd;
books, Breviary, one wooden desk;

one Mexican candlestick, one stone
Celtic Cross and one dark green
glass Shamrock—made in China.

All the rest has blended with the wind.

EPILOGUE

Which Way?

Ride a green wave out to sea and be gone
or plant waves of green and settle on land.
These were my choices that summer dawn
when I stood on the sun-buttered shore,
looking out, looking back, doubly drawn.

I was straining to leave; I longed to remain.
Someone had told me of oceans that sing
and broad fields that shine when it rains.
Each way was even, like butterflies' wings.
Desperate, I asked myself an old question:
To others, which gifts would I want to bring?
The reply, unexpected, was simply *"Words."*
I paced, stunned, unsure of this offering.

At times you don't choose your direction;
A direction can swerve to make its choice.
I was not called to sea or to farmland.
On the writer's trail, I found my own voice.
I hear it still and I'm still on that trail;
now words are children I'm able to hoist.
I listened to life and life led me here—
poor but rich, nothing rued, I rejoice.

NOTES:

On the Author::

Marcy Heidish is an award-winning author of sixteen books of fiction, non-fiction and poetry. Her first novel, *A WOMAN CALLED MOSES*, was made into a television movie starring Cicely Tyson.

She is the recipient of a National Endowment for the Arts Creative Writing Fellowship Grant, a L.I.N.K.S. Award, a Schubert Fellowship, a finalist for an "Edgar" Award, and other honors.

Ms. Heidish has taught at Georgetown University, The George Washington University, Howard University, and Fordham University. She has conducted numerous writing workshops and seminars.

In addition, Ms. Heidish has been a long-term volunteer in shelters for homeless women, a volunteer on a hotline, a hospice, and the Lighthouse for the Blind.

Born in New York City and a long-time resident of Washington, D.C., Marcy Heidish now lives and writes in Colorado.

~~~~~

On the Text:

• Most of these poems are new. Some, specially selected, were previously published in *Too Late To Be A Fortune Cookie Writer* and *Burning the Maid: Poems for Joan of Arc* both by Marcy Heidish.

• The Italian word *ecco* means "here" or "here it is."

• A dip-pen could have been made of oak.

<u>Critical Acclaim For Novels By Marcy Heidish</u>

A WOMAN CALLED MOSES

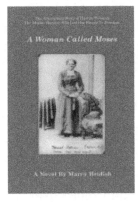

*Award-winning, best-selling novel based on the life of Harriet Tubman, abolitionist and conductor on the Underground Railroad.

*Literary Guild Alternate Selection;
*A Bantam paperback.

*TV Movie, starring Cicely Tyson, still available on DVD.

*Houghton Mifflin Co., 1ˢᵗ Pub.

<u>Praise for *A Woman Called Moses*</u>:

Publishers Weekly: "Her story has been told before, but never as eloquently, almost poetically, as here...achingly real...a strong narrative of a totally committed woman, one who speaks directly to our own desperate need to feel committed—and our wish that somewhere in the world there were more people like Harriet Tubman."

Washington Post Book World: "Profoundly rewarding...a daring work of the imagination."

Chicago Sun Times: "Marcy Heidish has, almost uncannily, crawled into the skin and very mind of Harriet Tubman. The dialogue sings with poetic beauty."

Houghton Mifflin Co.: "As events build toward a stunning climax, we are drawn into the spellbinding narrative of an extraordinary life, and a portion of our American past."

WITNESSES

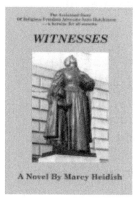

* Award-winning novel based on the life of lay minister Anne Hutchinson, America's first female advocate of religious freedom.

* Citations: Society for Colonial Wars; laudatory reviews; large-print, hard-cover and paperback versions.

* **Houghton Mifflin Co., 1ˢᵗPub.**

Praise for *Witnesses:*

The New York Times Book Review: "...nothing ordinary about her creation of this remarkable woman. The novel abounds in literary grace. It employs the voices of the times as though heard this minute."

The New Yorker Magazine: "A striking novel...a compelling portrait."

The Washington Post: "Pure pleasure. Anne Hutchinson is real; thanks to *Witnesses,* she at last assumes her proper place in American history." —Jonathan Yardley, Pulitzer Prize-winning critic.

Ballantine Books: "This fearless woman, mother of fifteen, a leader in medicine and politics, comes to vivid life in these pages. A true believe in religious freedom who paid dearly for her principles in two trials for heresy. In the tradition of Arthur Miller's *The Crucible*, Witnesses is the deeply felt portrait of a woman in the paranoid climate of 17ᵗʰ century Boston."

THE TORCHING—The Book Store Murders

* Acclaimed contemporary novel, in hardcover and paperback.
* Literary Guild Alternate Selection; laudatory reviews.
* Optioned for TV movie.

* **Simon & Schuster, 1ˢᵗ Pub.**

Praise for _The Torching_:

Washington Post Book World: "Because of Heidish's skill, we get the full force of her double-whammy, in part due to the grace with which she weaves the present-day and the historical, but also because of her inventiveness at the book's close, the daring way she gets both strands of plot to unite... a stylish and intelligent novelist to boot, more than up to the dizzying, tale-spinning task that she set for herself here."
Kirkus Reviews: "Shuddery mystery-suspense with supernatural overtones."
Library Journal: "Intricately constructed. A deliciously spine-tingling, multi-layered literary mystery."
Publishers Weekly: "Subtle, gratifying psychological suspense. Penetrating characterizations...Heidish impeccably orchestrates the historical and contemporary, the supernatural and psychological."
Denver Post: "Macabre ride...Eerie. Intriguing. Frightening surprises...Enjoy."
Arizona Daily Star: "An imaginative, amazing writer...A magician with words."
New York Daily News: "Compellingly readable and likely to induce the screaming-meemies."

THE SECRET ANNIE OAKLEY

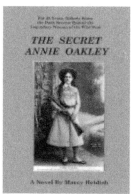

* Acclaimed novel based on the life of the legendary sharp-shooter.
* Hard- and Paperback versions
* A *Readers Digest* Condensed Novel.
* Optioned for film.
*Translated into several languages, laudatory reviews.

*New American Library, 1ˢᵗ Pub.

Praise for *The Secret Annie Oakley:*

Kirkus Reviews: "An immensely touching and cohesive fictional biography of the legendary sharp-shooter, builds from exemplary research to a fresh portrait of a talented woman in crisis, a class act—as Heidish reconstructs. with color and drama, the choreography of the shows, the tone of the period, and the textures of a haunting past."

The Arizona Daily Star: "...an imaginative, amazing writer, a magician with words. Each character has been brought to life with a mere pen stroke; flesh and blood beings that are more than fiction. A master-piece of creative writing."

The Kansas City Star: "An unforgettable story."

Christian Science Monitor: "...Marcy Heidish weaves historical facts into a novel so moving that there will be many times in the years to come that I'll take pleasure in remembering that stout-hearted woman. 'Annie Oakley' hits the bull's eye every time."

MIRACLES

MIRACLES

A Novel By Marcy Heidish

* Historical novel based on the life of **Mother Elizabeth Seton**, first American-born canonized saint.

* Main selection, *The Catholic Book Club*.

*New American Library, 1st Pub.

Praise for *Miracles*:

The New York Times Book Review: "This appealing book, told from the point of view of a skeptical modern priest, moves swiftly through tragedy to triumph."

Kirkus Reviews: "Working delicately with a balance of Church hagiography and psychological insight, Ms. Heidish provides another strong focus on the root dilemma of female saints and achievers."

New American Library: "*Miracles* is the story of an unforgettable woman's life and love. It is a novel charged with the vitality of a life that saw many changes, and with the power of a love that took many forms.[whether] as a lonely daughter of a wealthy, indifferent man; a searching young woman; a contented matron embracing a marriage that produced five beloved children; a widow searching for new meaning to life."

DEADLINE

* Contemporary psychological novel with a "mystery" as a narrative line.

* Nominee for prestigious national "Edgar" Award; fine reviews.

* St. Martin's Press, 1ˢᵗ Pub.

Praise for Deadline:

Washington Post: "Deadline is a tense, well-turned tale, filled with authentic police and newspaper people. Heidish's taut, punchy style moves the story at lightning speed."

Kirkus Reviews: "The high-tension plot is enhanced by sharply etched pictures, by many vivid characters, and by a crisp, clean, first-person style. Heidish imbues her haunting story and her gutsy heroine with a rare sense of tenderness and poignancy. An impressive mystery by a gifted writer."

St. Martin's Press: "This wire-tight novel probes relentlessly, driving deep into psychological darkness and violent death. As the riveting story reaches its stunning conclusion, we see a complex woman forced to meet the ultimate deadline."

A Dangerous Woman: Mother Jones, An Unsung American Heroine

*A compelling, inspiring new historical novel, another powerful "profile in courage" American-style novel based on the life of Mary Harris Jones, a self-proclaimed Hell Raiser, daring labor leader, and colorful, quirky humanitarian.

*The arresting novel of an indomitable force, dressed demurely in widow's weeds and lace collars who:

> As an Irish immigrant—lost her homeland to the Great Famine.

> As a wife and mother—lost her whole family to yellow fever.

> As a dressmaker—lost home and business to the Chicago Fire

> As a survivor—turned from sorrow to help others survive.

Follow one of America's most feisty, fearless and forgotten heroines whose rallying cry was:

"PRAY FOR THE DEAD—AND FIGHT LIKE HELL FOR THE LIVING!"

DESTINED TO DANCE: A Novel About Martha Graham

> They called her a genius.
> They called her a goddess.
> They called her a monster.
Which title best fits Martha Graham, iconic Mother of Modern Dance? Find out—in the <u>first historical novel about this great American diva.</u>

DESTINED TO DANCE is a creative portrait of the legendary dancer and choreographer. Heidish offers another remarkable account of an American heroine: her successes, her sorrows, and her struggles.

Here is a masterful portrait of Graham, on stage, backstage, offstage. We see Graham's break-through brilliance, often compared to Picasso's or Stravinsky.

We also witness Graham's triumph over alcoholism, despair, and a failed marriage. Set against the intriguing world of dance, Martha Graham's story offers us a close-up on a complex and compelling overcomer.

Martha Graham (1894-1991) invented a new "language of movement," still taught around the world and exemplified in such classic works as *Appalachian Spring*, among 180 others.

As always, Heidish's research is thorough and her sense of her subject is magical. For all who love the arts, all who seek inspiration, and all who like to read between history's lines, *DESTINED TO DANCE* is a must-read book.

Scene Through A Window
A Historical Romance

Travel through the centuries to watch a timeless love unfold around a timeless masterpiece: the fabled cathedral of Chartres, France. In 1194, an unthinkable disaster struck that sacred site. In one June night, a firestorm devastated the cathedral, its artwork, and parts of its surrounding town.

Immediately, the finest artists converged on Chartres to plan a new and innovative structure, built to endure and to surpass all that went before. Inevitably, these plans led to plots and rivalry, threatening the realization of a daring and demanding dream.

Against this backdrop, two lovers struggle to conceive the new cathedral's stained glass windows, still regarded as marvels today. This quest centers on discovering <u>new gem-like colors:</u> unique, precious, and <u>incomparable.</u> The pair, under increasing pressure, embarks on an intense search for the mysterious but elusive answers

Deftly weaving fact with fiction, Marcy Heidish sets an inspirational love story against a thoroughly researched Medieval backdrop. With her proven attention to detail, Heidish transports us to the winding streets of Chartres: its sounds and smells, its interiors and intrigues. Suspenseful, engrossing, and imaginative, *Scene Through A Window* creates a magical space where the impossible can happen.

Soul and the City
WaterBrook Press, Random House imprint

Praise for *Soul and the City*:

*"I actually started reading Marcy Heidish's *Soul and the City* on a subway train. I must say it had exactly the effect she writes about: it gave me peace in the middle of the hurry, the rush, the loud noise of the city."
—Rick Hamlin, executive editor, Guideposts; author of *Finding God on the A Train*

* "Marcy Heidish has compiled a rich and nuanced touring companion to rival any Michelin or Eye-witness guide—usable in any city of the world. Keep it close and you will meet beauty and holiness no matter where you pause to look."
— Leigh McLeroy, author of *The Beautiful Ache* and *The Sacred Ordinary*

* "*Soul and the City* is a deeply inspiring call to awareness to connection with God and with others, and ultimately to soulful worship through so many aspects of life in the city that we find mundane, undesirable, or that even go unnoticed. Almost instantly, upon delving into its pages, you find your perspective changed."
— Sarah Zacharias Davis, author of *Confessions from an Honest Wife, Transparent, and The Friends We Keep.*

Defiant Daughters
Liguori Publications.

A Candle At Midnight
Ave Maria Press, first publisher

Praise for *A Candle At Midnight*:

* "Heidish honors modern medicine and spiritual healing in this compelling work."

— Alen J. Salerian, M.D., Medical Director of the Washing-ton Psychiatric Center

* "This is not a book of abstractions. I recommend this book to anyone who is caught in the darkness of mid-night."

— Martha Manning, Author of *Undercurrents: A Life Beneath the Surface*:

* "A masterpiece!"

— Rev. Nancy Eggert, Spiritual Director

Who Cares? Simple Ways YOU Can Reach Out
Ave Maria Press, first publisher

Praise for *Who Cares?*:
A lonely neighbor, a colleague in distress, a friend in difficulty. In situations like these we want to reach out and help, yet so often we feel unsure about our response.

What to do?
What to say?
What is enough?
Too much?
Too little?

This practical book is designed to bring out the caring person in each of us. Marcy Heidish offers simple, specific ways to practice the art of caring, especially within our immediate circle of concern: family, friends, neighbors, and coworkers.

Heidish reminds us of the many little things we can do to open the door to a caring relationship.

— **Ave Maria Press**

"Contains savvy insights and wisdom about service. This is an ideal resource for anyone interested in engaged spirituality."

— *Cultural Information Service*

Too Late To Be A Fortune Cookie Writer
"A novelist has a specific poetic license which also applies to his own life."
~ Jerzi Kosinski

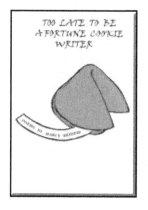

Marcy Heidish, award-winning author of fourteen books, fiction and non-fiction, is just such a novelist with a "specific poetic license."

Her work has been praised for its "lyrical grace" and so it is a special joy to present her first book of poetry. Ms. Heidish has written poems for decades.

With humor and humanity, this collection spans a broad range of subjects. Insight, wit and depth enliven these poems. They address universal concerns: maturity, mortality, memory and much more.

Ms. Heidish gives us an intimate glimpse into a writer's soul. Adept at varied verse forms, she amuses, reflects, recalls, and rejoices:

• "A watched pot never boils unless you're boiling vodka."

• "Houses crowd my life like chairs on a November beach."

• "The sun is a peach, half ripened, at hand." And the poet brings us with her.

BURNING THE MAID:
POEMS FOR JOAN OF ARC

"Joan was a being so uplifted from the ordinary run of mankind that she finds no equal in a thousand years....Her story would be beyond belief if it were not true."
—Winston Churchill

"She is the Wonder of the Ages. And when we consider her origin, her early circumstances, her sex, and that she did all the things upon which her renown rests while she was a young girl, we recognize that while our race continues, she will also be the Riddle of the Ages."
—Mark Twain

Here, in poetry, is a fresh approach to Joan of Arc, that famous heroine-for-all-seasons. Almost six hundred years after she was burned at the stake, Joan's story still compels, fascinates and challenges us.

Credited with saving France, that famous warrior-maid leaps from a new poetry collection by Marcy Heidish, a gifted specialist in historical fiction (*A Woman Called Moses, Destined to Dance,* etc). Heidish's poetic reflections on Joan are riveting, imaginative, and beautifully crafted.

Whether you know a little or a lot about Joan of Arc, this original and elegant collection will invite you to see "The Maid of Orleans" from a wealth of insightful perspectives. If you approach Joan as a role model, a puzzle, or a poem herself, you will find this book an impressive and inspiring read.

Short Pieces:

Articles and book reviews published in *Ms.* Magazine, *GEO* Magazine, *The Washington Post*, *The Washington Star*, and various in-flight periodicals.

Two of these pieces are:

* ***The Pilgrim Who Stayed***, *GEO* Magazine, about Chartres Cathedral, widely translated.

* ***The Grand Dame of the Harbor***, about the Statue of Liberty, was a highly acclaimed cover story for *GEO* Magazine. This article is included in a textbook anthology designed to teach writing to college students. Winner of coveted Apex Award.

See Marcy Heidish page at:

www.Amazon.com

[AND Kindle] *

www.marcyheidishbooks.com

* Marcy Heidish Books are printed by Lightning Source and distributed by Ingram of Ingram Content Group Inc., the world's largest distributor of physical and digital content, providing books, music and media content to over 38,000 retailers, libraries, schools and distribution partners in 195 countries. More than 25,000 publishers use Ingram's.

INDEX

CPSIA information can be obtained at www.ICGtesting.com
Printed in the USA
BVOW06s1141310116

434431BV00017B/80/P

9 780990 526247